# Love Your Light

## Poetry to Inspire

Love Your Light

Poetry to Inspire

Some of these poems first appeared in We Are One,

and Know Your Way chapbooks.

Cover art by Sarah Mauri, 2023.

Second edition.

Published by Four Wild Geese Design, Mount Shasta, California 96067

ISBN 978-1-7324373-5-7

**Dedicated
to my
mom,
Donna Chambley
August 9, 1944-May 30, 2015**

# Contents

## Love Your Light

The Sun is the heart
of all that is.

Our heart is a Sun--
shining, sparkling
lighting our path.

## *The Night Has a Thousand Eyes*
### *Frances William Bourdillian, 1899*

*The night has a thousand eyes,*
*   And the day but one:*
*Yet the light of the bright world dies*
*   With the dying sun.*

*The mind has a thousand eyes,*
*   And the heart but one:*
*Yet the light of a whole life dies*
*   When love is done.*

# Alpha & Omega

The Sun never dies---
Alpha and Omega--
the beginning and the end,
male and female.

Many and the One--
tiny and infinitesimal.

Dark and light--
absence.
Night.

A thousand ways to say
I love you
Yet only one
is needed.

A thousand sperm swimming
competition.
Yet only one
Wins.

I see clearer
with my eyes shut--
light inside
the brightest.

Is love ever done?
Where is the beginning
and the end--
Alpha and Omega.

Do you remember your first love?
School girl crush.
Innocent.
Why does it always end
different
than it begins?

My heart is a flame---
like Calcifer, a friendly fire spirit--
sometimes small,
confined, burning blue
othertimes explosive
bright orange bonfire
reaching high, sparks
into black night.
Can you see my spark?
Feel my heat?

Be a clean love.
Burn clearly.
Begin and end the same.
See it through.
Alpha and Omega.

## Light

I walk in the light---I Am the light.

I shine my light for all to see.

I join the light of my family.

I ride the Rainbow Bridge to my home.

My home is bright---

My father is the Sun.

I have been 'born' on the Mother.

She is returning to the Light.

We are all Light.

## Solar Flash

The moon winks,
dozes, Zzzzz
while planets
swirl in orbit.
Our Sol Star
glowing Super
Nova.

The flora and fauna
will swoon--
sway,
when the Daystar
makes its
appearance.

The Solar wind brings us
Gift packages,
a sonic shower
of protons, electrons--
Coronal Stream.

This is the year,
the Grand Event--
Solar Flash.

## Walking the Way of Wisdom

Detach---
Be the observer.

Be like the White Knight---
he walks in kindness and compassion.

Compassion
is purity in action.

See the beauty in all perspectives.

Expect a view
that is different than yours.

Be open to New Ways
of doing, thinking, expressing---

We are beautiful in our uniqueness.
Appreciate that variety.

Allow Free Will
the space
to expand.

## Grace

Atone.
Be at--one.
Flow into grace.
Bide your time here.
Save space in the tomb.
We are all born innocent.
Show you care.
Hug an Orca.
Be colorblind.
Aim for joy.
Romp the land.
Accept the gift.
Grace.

## Realizations

Lessons---
I've learned that if I treat a person---a certain way
that I will be treated the same way---by someone else.

Its ok--I love you.*

Someone told me on my bday---
"Your not old--your experienced."
I feel sad that I am old--
If I knew then, what I do now---
Would I, could I have done more?
To be 'experienced' and have youth and joy--
wouldn't that be cool?

Another friend told me--
"Don't sing---your voice is flat."
I feel sad, I didn't do more with music and art---
Learn, Practice and Do--
I love singing,
and I will keep on.
I feel sad,
I never learned to play an instrument or draw a picture.

Its ok--I love you.

My creative successes were around---
Furnishing a house, Feeding a family on a budget.
My energy was spent--
raising kids
making ends meet.
That has been my whole life---
when married, I added the role of peacemaker.

So many lessons, so much sadness.
Its ok--I love you.

In the night, grief finds me.
I wanted to travel, give talks, hold workshops---
I was told 'Play in your own back yard'.

Its ok--I love you.

Now,
I do what I know--
I keep it simple--
I live in my own reality.
I give myself--
love and acceptance.
Its ok--I love you.

*J.H.

## Faded Rose

'Listen to the call of lightning and rain
Wash away the pain of love that's lost.'*
Lost slipper, crown and halo--
Will Prince Charming ever come?

Wash away the pain of love that's lost.
Could it be a faded rose from days gone by.
Will Prince Charming ever come?
Imprisoned in your self made coma.

Could it be a faded rose from days gone by.
Till the ground, plant new seeds--
Imprisoned in your self made coma.
Prom Queen give up your throne.

Till the ground, plant new seeds--
Loose the slipper, crown and halo.
Prom Queen give up your throne.
Listen to the call of lightning and rain.

*Jan Dorrell

## Take 2

Release your inner genie.
Welcome to the cosmic
Fold.
No time to hide---
Come out of the closet.

Take 22
Do you believe in fate?
Is this a play
we keep re-living?

Take 44
Don't mean to be 'blunt'---- But,
Face the Sun--
It is your healing.
Day by day.

Take 50
Why am I awake at this time?

Take 66
Many tries---
Do something different---

Hope for New--
I want a new me!

Take 70
I sit with White Buffalo Calf Woman---
Remember the passing
of the sacred chanuka---
Cherishing the trinkets
I have gathered.

Take 78
I honor my ancestors--
they come in different forms---
Some have feathers, others fur,
and still others like the 2 legged of today.

Take 82
My pipe will carry me
to the places of before.

Take 89
I am the wild boar,
rustling the ground with my nose--

Take 90
I am a startled deer,
listening for danger.

91
I am Hawk meeting the sunset.
A cougar feeding her young.

Take 99
Insomnia again---
This is when the story ends.
Tomorrow is a new day!

# Life is What You Make It

Can't fall asleep---
while the god of thunder
is pounding.

What a grave gambit.
Will the true Oz
Please stand Up--
Please stand Up?

Clap! Yay!
Another day--
another argument averted.
A sacred rite
saves the day.
The Way of the dove--
Peace Ritual.
It starts as a feeling---
becomes a knowing--
deep in your bones.

Who gets your praise?
Do you believe in the one true god?
You and I are God--
it's only hidden
in plain sight.

Feeling stress?
Take it down a notch--
There is no lien on this life--
only what you give up.
You can bank on that.

"No worries".
Play like children.
Have fun.
Party at my house!

## Stomp that ant

Words left unsaid
become stones in stomach.
'If I say nothing, do I exist?'*
Be strong, kind and bold.

Muddy stones in stomach.
Thoughts lay heavy on my heart.
Be strong, kind and bold.
Dirt swept under a rug.

Thoughts lay heavy on my heart.
To hell with the rules.
Dirt swept under a rug.
Stomp that ant with heavy boot.

To hell with the rules
If I say nothing, do I exist?
Stomp that ant with heavy boot.
Words left unsaid.

*Megan Peralta

## SoCal vs NorCal *

In SoCal
they drink
Kelp and Banana juice---

Play ping pong--
and skate boarding
is a legitimate means of transport.

Sexy girls
wear red roses
in their hair---
soft skin,
flash of boob.

Goth porn
is free at the bus stop.

In NorCal
they eat
greasy fries
smothered in sauce.

Ride the bus for free--

Wear brightly colored wigs
like smurfs, strawberry shortcake
or some other lost cartoon of the 70's.

You can play dice or pool
at the local Weed lounge---
and chains are required for travel.

Boots are worn--
and frisbee is a serious sport.

Names are changed on a whim---
and the wise man wears a robe.

*We all wish for summer.

## Pica

She likes to eat
the flap of envelopes,
especially the sticky part,
the way it feels on her tongue.

In Kindergarten,
Art was her favorite--
because she loved paste--
the consistency, texture, taste.
Mushy like Mr. Puffinstuff.

Now, she settles
for bean burritos
no onions or red sauce.

## Cake

Be on the verge--

Eat prune cake for breakfast
with a cherry on top.

Toss a coin--
each coin toss is a fiat--
test of faith.

Play a new tune
Nay
The beat goes on---
Ring the bell, but

don't leave your drool
on the door.

Nothing matters--
so don't worry.

Eat prune cake for breakfast.

## Job Interview

Why bother?
It's not a paying gig--

Perhaps---
We can barter.

Trade time--
I'll give you mine
if you give me yours.

Don't just fade away--
without a trace.

No road to travel--
No place to go--

Nothing to prove.
Cat got your tongue?
Take it back.

film, film, film
Keep on rolling--
down the river.

Lend me your eyes and ears--
Won't cost you a cent--

Go where your needed--
Cancel the Karma.
Show all mercy---
more so yourself.

Take a dose of
Fukitol (fuck it all),
and call me in the morning.

Never mind--
Don't call us,
We'll call you.

## What is Your Weather Like?

Mother Earth's
    Clean up team---

Wind, Rain and Snow
Wiping the slate clean.

Rein in your anger--
Rain.

Shout---
Pelt like hail.
Let it all out---

Release the dam you've built.
Flood--
of tears.

Blow like a blizzard.
The whistling wind
clears the way.

Nature shows us how.

## Grandfather Tree Park

Some protect the forest, some fight fires---

Others call trees logs---
and take them away from their home.

Parks are safe places
from loggers and the Mill---
where people and trees
can be at peace.

My heart sits in awe--
of their unique beauty, firm resolve
and quiet strength.

## Everything Happens for a Reason

Elk roam the winter woods--
while
a dragon sleeps.

Why does the winter tree
leave her nuts behind?

To start anew,
Begin again,
Grow Green
All over.

Branch Out.

There is a time and a season
for everything under the sun.

Do you know what season it is?

Time for healing.
Quail cozy by moonlight.
Trees dance.
It is your fate to heal.

Spring begins anew.

## Rainbow

I will not be an ostrich
with her head buried
in shame. Ostracized.

I will not be invisible.

I will not feel guilty
for being myself.

I will not give up--
Run and hide.

I will not take things personal.
I will allow others their way.

Remembering---
We all shine
a bit differently.
Together we are the full spectrum--

Rainbow.

## Puzzle

Everyone loves a puzzle.

There's meaning behind everything--
until there isn't.

>Tri-ath-a-lon
>trial of the body.
>Go the distance.
>End--
>Where you are.

Sometimes,
the meaning
is just plain being.

## Tao of Life

Once a year,
I meet my ex for lunch--
We have tofu Ziti, lentils
and fake champagne.

I leave my hash jar
in the car.

Be good.
Give it a try.
You'll surprise yourself.

In this life,
adversity is the cost--
What are you willing to pay?

It's like an entrance fee
for
the contest of life.

What is the prize?
The complete and utter
Satisfaction--
of a job well done!

It starts as a feeling,
becomes a knowing--
deep in your bones.

Walk in integrity.
You just know--
Your Right
Way.

The Tao of Life
Varies--
For each person
must choose their
path.

## I Don't Keep Score

I am not athletic--I don't do yoga.
I'm not excited for ski season--
you won't catch me on a
surfboard.

I don't do the gym thing--
chlorinated pools, hot tubs
and locker room showers.

I am not fond of all nite events--
bars, concerts or parties.

I am not my mother--
that takes work.
Good for you, Cheryl!

I don't rely on the medical profession,
to tell me about my health.
I don't need to try out the latest
surgery or pharmaceutical
to feel complete.

I no longer hop
from one addiction to another--
sex, alcohol, shopping.

I'm not a Martha Stewart type,
my ducks are not all in a row.

I am not famous--
ballerina, race car driver
or a world traveler.

I don't follow the Dow, politics
or my local representative.

I'm not angry anymore,
I don't blame others
for my life.

It is so much more fun
when you don't keep score.

## Traffic Jam

Ever hit a traffic jam
in the maze of life?

Take time to sit
with your jam.
Sync.

Don't equate things
with time--

Give of yourself
to yourself.

I don't know the words to this song.
Voices enter--
the void.

If you hear them,
you can follow.
Trust enough--
to follow.

## Making Music

The great oxen yodels--
Mice climb up high
to see.

They hope to leave their jail---someday.

The song triggers--
a genetic explosion
internal firing
multiple orgasms
fireworks.

Divas dream. Flowers bloom. Mice play.

We will find a way.

Bring zeal
to your song.
Sing like a diva--
deliver with zing!

## Thor Visits Mid-Gard

Sky darkens like war.
Golden gates crash open---
the Old Ones return.


## Muddy

At the water line---
Reeds stand attention,
wasp and spiders dance.

## How many eggs in your basket?

How many eggs in your basket?
My basket overflows.
'I am not a hero--
one egg is not enough.'*

My basket overflows.
Field of Easter eggs and daffodils.
One egg is not enough.
Tinkerbell come out and play.

Field of Easter eggs and daffodils.
I wonder why the bluebird sings--
Tinkerbell come out and play.
Poets long dead await.

I wonder why the bluebird sings--
A call for love, long lost.
Poets long dead await.
Our words, our hopes, our dreams.

A call for love, long lost.
I am not a hero.
Our words, our hopes, our dreams.
How many eggs in your basket?

*Rita Chambers

# Freedom

The three sisters
named the game
Fate.

Dive off a steep reef--
Meet a herd of dolphin.
Be a friend, not foe.

Hope to climb back up--
Toad on a sugarcane stalk.

Toads and pixies play together.
Ring around the posie.

Daisies grow best in sandy soil.

A mage,
better known as the wiz--
plays a jute
while nude
girls, girls, girls
are ready for fun.

Slaves make speedy escape--
while a woolly dog wanders in fog,
no longer guarding the crew--

Mutiny. Run away. Exodus.

No more daily grind--
Put away your mop and broom.

Eagles fly free.

Trial of the century--
Pivotal day in court.
Human beings
Set free.

## Peace Offering

I am offering this poem...

as a guide, a few words to
take you there.

a peace offering,
apology for my shortfalls.

a chocolate,
round, dark, soft
filled with peppermint.

as a mirror,
held up to each other.

as a drum,
to beat your own rhythm.

as a gift,
part of myself,
a quick introduction
of who I am.

as a playground,
merry-go-round
hold on tight, swing, slide--
Play.

as a sacred, tribal headpiece--
connection to the ancestors,
as a peace pipe,
Respect.

a timeship, travel
to all timelines--
past, present and future.

as my final performance,
Retiring--
One last concert to remember me by.

The End

About the author---

Cheryl Lunar Wind lives in the Mount Shasta area in a little town called Weed. She is a practicer of Mayan cosmology, Lakota ceremony, Star Knowledge and the Universal Laws including the Law of One. Her hobbies are writing poetry, music, dance, drum circles and love for all life; plant, animal and crystal. Cheryl has been a guide and spiritual teacher for many years. Now she shares wisdom and wit through poetry, and has published poetry books; Know Your Way, We Are One, Follow the White Rabbit and Love Your Light.

www.ingramcontent.com/pod-product-compliance
Lightning Source LLC
Chambersburg PA
CBHW060644030426
42337CB00018B/3437